Let's discuss

ENERGY RESOURCES

Nuclear Power

WITHDRAWN

Richard and Louise Spilsbury

WAYLAND

First published in 2015 by Wayland

Copyright © Wayland 2015

Dewey number: 333.7'924-dc22
ISBN: 978 0 7502 9451 5
Library eBook: 978 0 7502 7291 9

10 9 8 7 6 5 4 3 2 1

MIX
Paper from
responsible sources
FSC® C104740
www.fsc.org

Editorial director: Rasha Elsaeed
Produced for Wayland by Discovery Books Ltd
Managing editor: Rachel Tisdale
Designer: Ian Winton
Illustrator: Stefan Chabluk
Picture researcher: Tom Humphrey

Picture credits: Corbis: 13 (Roger Ressmeyer), 15 (Dominique Aubert/Sygma), 22 (Yang Liu); Exelon: cover main; FOM-Institute 27 (FOM-Institute for Plasma Physics Rijnhuizen, Association EURATOM-FOM); Getty Images: 8 bottom (Emory Kristof/ National Geographic), 17 (Dimitar Dilkoff/AFP), 25 (Carsten Koall), 28 (Wang Lei/ ChinaFotoPress); Nuclear Innovation North America LLC: imprint page & 11; Shutterstock: cover background (Panos Karapanagiotis), 12 (Marcin Balcerzak), 19 (Steve Cukrov), 24 (Tomasz Bidermann); Wikimedia: title page & 4 (marya), 8 top (Ikiwaner), 14 (Pacific Northwest National Laboratory), 16 (Justin Stahlman), 18 (Bill Gillette), 20 (Nuclear Regulatory Commission), 23 (kallerna).

Wayland
An imprint of
Hachette Children's Group
Part of Hodder & Stoughton
Carmelite House
50 Victoria Embankment
London EC4Y 0DZ

Printed in China

An Hachette UK company
www.hachette.co.uk
www.hachettechildrens.co.uk

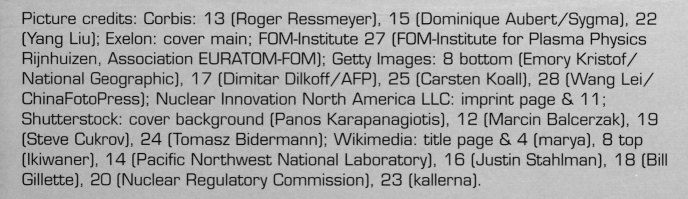

Contents

The words in **bold** can be found in the glossary on page 31.

Nuclear power as an energy resource

Energy resources are important, because they help us to do work. For example, we burn gas in stoves to cook food and use wind energy to move a yacht. Nuclear power harnesses energy released during **reactions** in nuclear fuel. Most **nuclear energy** is used to generate electricity in power stations, but it is also used to power spacecraft and submarines.

Electricity today

About two-thirds of electricity used globally today is generated from **fossil fuels** using the energy created from burning fuels such as coal and gas. But burning these fuels releases **greenhouse gases** like carbon dioxide, which trap heat in the **atmosphere** and cause **global warming**. The other gases cause air **pollution**. Fossil fuels are also running out because they are finite or **non-renewable**. This means no more are being formed to replace what is being used up.

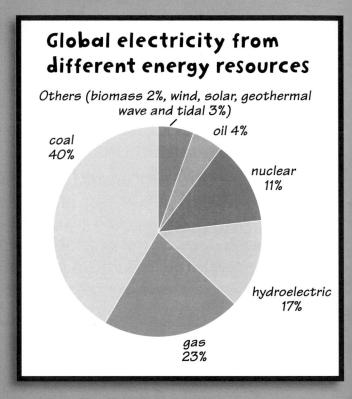

Global electricity from different energy resources

Others (biomass 2%, wind, solar, geothermal wave and tidal 3%)

coal 40%

oil 4%

nuclear 11%

hydroelectric 17%

gas 23%

Renewable power

Around 22 per cent of global electricity is generated using **renewable** resources, which will not run out. The most widely used renewables are hydroelectric, which uses the force of moving water, and biomass, which uses plant fuels. However, wind, solar, tidal, wave and geothermal (heat from underground) resources are also important. None are as polluting as fossil fuels.

The Diablo Canyon nuclear power station, California, USA, supplies electricity for over 3 million people using energy from nuclear fuel.

The nuclear option

The remaining electricity used around the world comes from nuclear power stations. Some countries, such as Norway or Nigeria, do not use nuclear power, but others, including France and Slovakia, generate most of their electricity from it. Nuclear power releases lots of energy from a small amount of fuel without greenhouse gases. However, the biggest problem with nuclear power is the hazardous **radiation** its waste can produce (see page 12).

Nuclear power around the world

North America

Europe

Asia

Middle East

Africa

South America

Oceania

Australia

Most nuclear power stations are in Europe, North America and Japan. This map shows the distribution of nuclear power stations in 2009.

Why discuss nuclear power?

In the future, countries will need to generate more of the electricity they need without using fossil fuels. This is because they want to slow global warming, but also meet electricity demand when these fuels start to run out or become unavailable due to political problems between countries. Where renewables are not being developed fast enough to meet demand, the best available option may be nuclear power. This book explores how nuclear power works, and its advantages and disadvantages compared with other energy resources now and in the years to come.

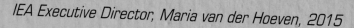

'Nuclear energy remains the second-largest source of low-carbon electricity worldwide. And, indeed, if we are to meet our collective climate goals, nuclear energy is critical.'

IEA Executive Director, Maria van der Hoeven, 2015

What is nuclear energy?

Nuclear energy is found inside **atoms** of nuclear fuel. When a fuel atom splits in two, the energy is released as heat. When large numbers of atoms split at the same time, enormous quantities of heat are produced.

Releasing energy from atoms

Everything in the world is made up of atoms. These are so small that four million could fit side-by-side on a pinhead! Most of any atom is made up of space through which tiny particles called electrons move fast. At the centre of an atom is a **nucleus** packed with tiny parts, or particles, called protons and **neutrons**. The protons all have a positive charge. This should push them apart, just as the like poles of magnets repel each other. However, the particles are held together instead by a strong nuclear force.

The nuclei of certain types of atom such as **uranium** can split in a process called **nuclear fission**. Nuclear fission happens during a reaction when the atoms are hit with a stream of moving neutrons. The nuclear energy is then released as heat. When one nucleus splits, it releases neutrons that can split other nuclei, and so on. This type of reaction that keeps itself going is called a **chain reaction**. The nuclear chain reaction produces lots of heat.

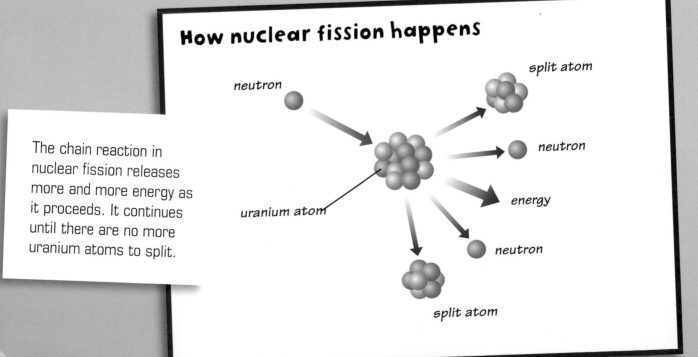

How nuclear fission happens

neutron

split atom

neutron

energy

uranium atom

neutron

split atom

The chain reaction in nuclear fission releases more and more energy as it proceeds. It continues until there are no more uranium atoms to split.

Bombs to power stations

Scientists first discovered nuclear fission in the early 20th century. At first uncontrolled nuclear chain reactions were used to make nuclear bombs, not electricity. The USA developed and dropped two nuclear bombs on Japan with devastating results at the end of World War II. In the 1950s technology was developed to control the chain reaction so nuclear fuel could release heat gradually. This was first used to generate electricity in nuclear power stations in Russia and the USA, and also to power submarines. Now there are over 430 nuclear power stations in operation worldwide with around a further 70 in construction.

Let's discuss

Uranium is a better energy resource than coal

Advantages:

Energy rich
Uranium costs around 400 times the price of coal but is more energy-rich. A one-gram piece can release as much energy as burning 3 tonnes of coal.

No gases
Unlike fossil fuels, using nuclear fuel produces virtually no polluting or greenhouse gases, and does not speed up global warming.

Disadvantages:

Smaller amounts
There is enough uranium to last around 90 years at present rates of use, around half as long as predicted coal supplies.

Hazardous
Solid waste from nuclear fission is more hazardous to handle and dispose of than waste from fossil fuels.

Nuclear fuel is more energy-rich and, when hazardous waste is dealt with properly, better for the global environment than fossil fuels.

Nuclear fuel

Uranium is a metal found naturally in tiny amounts in rocks, soils, rivers and seas all around the world. It is mined only in places where there are larger amounts of it in rock called uranium ore. The uranium ore is then processed to create fuel for nuclear power stations.

Mining for uranium

Three-quarters of all uranium ore is dug up from underground mines and open pits on the surface, in the same way as coal miners extract coal from the Earth. In open-pit mines, miners use diggers and explosives to create wide holes in the ground and remove the uranium ore. The ore is then fed into crushing machines and the small pieces are dissolved in chemicals.

The Rossing uranium mine in Namibia is one of the largest open-pit uranium mines in the world.

The remaining quarter of all uranium is removed from the ground by **solution mining**. Miners drill holes into underground ore and pump chemicals through the rock to dissolve the uranium from it. The dissolved uranium can then be separated from other chemicals in the solution. This process creates a uranium-rich sludge that is dried to make **yellowcake**. Yellowcake is transported from mines to special factories that make nuclear fuel.

A worker tests the uranium content of yellowcake produced from uranium ore. One tonne of this ore produces around 2–5 kilograms of uranium after processing.

Known quantities or reserves of uranium ore are found worldwide, but in 2013 just two countries, Australia and Kazakhstan, provided over 40 per cent.

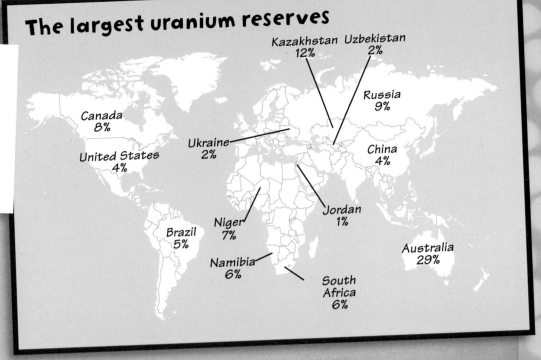

The largest uranium reserves

Kazakhstan 12%
Uzbekistan 2%
Russia 9%
Canada 8%
Ukraine 2%
China 4%
United States 4%
Jordan 1%
Niger 7%
Brazil 5%
Namibia 6%
South Africa 6%
Australia 29%

From uranium to fuel

Yellowcake is made up of two slightly different forms of uranium – over 99 per cent is Uranium 238 (U238) and less than 1 per cent is Uranium 235 (U235). However, U235 is the form that easily releases neutrons and is used for fission in nuclear power stations. Workers in nuclear fuel factories carefully heat the yellowcake to get rid of any impurities in the uranium. Then they put the uranium in special spinning machines to remove some of the U238. This process **enriches** the uranium, which means its proportion of U235 is increased. Finally, the enriched uranium is made into hard fuel pellets that are packed into bundles of metal tubes forming nuclear fuel rods. The fuel rods release very little radiation.

CASE STUDY
Uranium mining in Niger

Niger, Africa, is a poor, less-developed country and mining and selling uranium to nuclear power companies around the world is one of its most important industries. The major uranium mine in Niger and the second largest in the world is Imouraren. It is due to start production in 2015 after 6 years of development paid for partly by the Niger government and partly by the French nuclear company Areva. Imouraren's 179,000 tonnes of uranium ore should supply around 5,000 tonnes of yellowcake per year for about 35 years. Mine work will provide jobs for around 1,800 people on site and enhance the economy of the whole country.

How nuclear power stations work

The part of a nuclear power station where fission occurs is the **reactor**. Heat energy is transferred from the reactor into machinery that converts it into electrical energy.

From reactor to electricity

This is how the commonest type of nuclear reactor works.

1 *Reaction chamber:* Sealed steel vessel with hundreds of fuel rods arranged inside. Free neutrons released by U235 in the fuel start chain reactions in and between the rods. This releases more and more heat.

2 *Controlling the reaction:* **Control rods** are made of substances called boron or cadmium that absorb neutrons. They control the chain reaction in the U235. Machines in the reaction chamber move the control rods up or down between the fuel rods to speed up or slow down the reaction.

3 *Coolant:* The **coolant** carries the heat from the reaction chamber. As the coolant here is high-pressure water, this type of reactor is called a pressurized water reactor.

4 *Heat exchanger:* Heat from the coolant pipes warms water in the heat exchanger, making steam.

5 *Spinning in steam:* The steam blasts against a **turbine**, turning a shaft.

6 *Producing electricity:* The **generator** has coils of wire that spin between magnets to generate electricity.

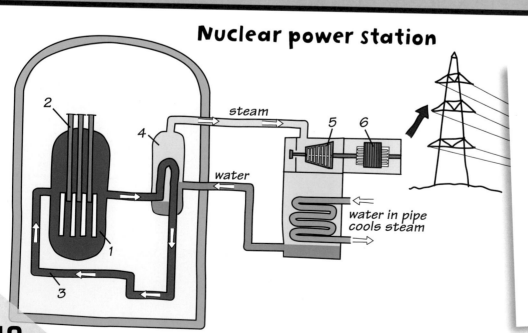

Nuclear power station

steam

water

water in pipe cools steam

In a nuclear power plant there are many energy conversions - nuclear to heat energy in the coolant, coolant heat to **kinetic energy** in steam, kinetic to **mechanical energy** in the turbine, and mechanical to electrical energy in the generator.

Water cooled

The steam that passes through the turbines is cooled so it **condenses** back into water before being heated up again in the heat exchanger or reaction chamber. Most nuclear power stations are built by rivers or by the sea and use water from these sources to cool the steam. Machines pump cold water from outside into pipes that pass through and condense the steam.

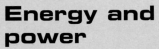

This is the view looking down onto a nuclear reactor within a tank of water for cooling. At the bottom you can just see the tops of the nuclear fuel and control rods.

Energy and power

Energy is the ability to do work, measured in joules. Power is the rate at which energy is used or sent, measured in watts or joules per second. A floor fan needs about 100 watts to work. An average nuclear power station generates about 1,000 million watts, or megawatts (MW), of electricity. This would provide enough electricity for a modern US city of up to one million people.

CASE STUDY · New Indian reactor

India has one of the fastest-growing populations in the world and a fast-developing economy demanding lots of electricity. The Bhabha Atomic Research Centre, Mumbai, is developing a new type of nuclear reactor to help meet this demand. This uses a mix of thorium, which is abundant in India, along with uranium, which is rarer. By supplying its own fuel, India is more self-sufficient in power production.

Radioactive waste

One of the big issues with nuclear power is that it produces hazardous waste. Nuclear waste is **radioactive** – it releases radiation comprising dangerous particles and invisible rays.

Radiation hazard

Strong radiation is hazardous to living things. It can, for example, cause burns or damage the structure of normal human body cells so they change into abnormal cancer cells. **Gamma rays** are the most dangerous radiation as they can easily pass through and affect normal body tissue, but radioactive particles are also a hazard when breathed in or swallowed. However, weak radiation is not hazardous. For example, most rocks and seawater contain small amounts of radioactive substances. Radiation is also safely used by doctors to locate medical problems or to cure cancers.

Spent fuel

Uranium fuel rods change into spent fuel as they release energy. The uranium changes into different substances. For example, some neutrons from U235 atoms join the U238 atoms and change them into **plutonium**. Spent fuel rods need to be replaced when they have lost most of their U235 because they no longer release enough heat in the reactor. However, substances left in the spent fuel continue to release high levels of gamma rays.

The waste needs to be carefully stored and handled to prevent this radiation from escaping.

A worker at a nuclear power station wears protective clothing while examining waste that could be radioactive.

Other waste

Used fuel is not the only radioactive waste. The coolant used to transfer heat from the reactor, clothing and tools used by workers in nuclear reactors, and building materials used to make reactors may all have dust on them that is contaminated with radioactive particles. Radioactive dust is a lower-level, longer-lasting hazard than spent fuel.

Workers use devices called Geiger counters to measure radioactivity, as here in a nuclear power station.

Let's discuss

Nuclear reactions create less waste than burning fossil fuels

For:

Small waste volume
A nuclear power station produces 20–25 tonnes of used fuel each year, whereas a coal power station produces around 500,000 tonnes of coal waste.

Radioactive fossil fuels
Some scientists say uranium in ash from numerous coal power stations creates a bigger radiation hazard than nuclear waste.

Against:

Health threat
People exposed to high levels of radiation from nuclear waste can develop cancers in different organs such as the lungs, skin and blood.

Long-term problem
High-level waste is intensely radioactive for tens of years, but low-level waste remains hazardous for thousands of years.

On balance, nuclear power produces far less waste than fossil fuel power, but the hazards of nuclear waste are more concentrated over longer periods.

Dealing with nuclear waste

Nuclear waste is either stored while it becomes less radioactive, sometimes over long periods, or **reprocessed** into fuel. Either way nuclear waste needs to be dealt with carefully to avoid release of radiation into the environment.

Storage

Waste fuel rods are first stored under water in special cooling ponds for several months to cool and slow the nuclear reactions. Then the waste fuel is usually chopped up, dissolved in strong chemicals and melted with glass fragments. The molten glass is poured into steel cylinders that are sealed before being encased in concrete barrels to prevent radiation from escaping. These barrels may be stored in strong, concrete buildings, such as old military camps or disused nuclear power stations, or deep underground. Some countries, such as the USA, use caves or old mines for high-level waste storage. Others, such as Finland, are digging special tunnels for this purpose. Lower-level waste is generally simply sealed in steel drums and left in surface waste dumps.

Molten, orange glass mixed with nuclear waste cools and hardens into black vitrified waste. Vitrification helps to prevent radiation from escaping from the waste.

Reprocessing

Spent fuel, unlike fossil fuel waste, can be recycled. Globally around 20 per cent of spent fuel is recycled by reprocessing. This process separates out the U235, which can be used to enrich more U238 for fuel, and also plutonium. Plutonium mixed with uranium can be used as fuel in some nuclear reactors called **fast-breeder reactors**.

There are just a few of these reactors worldwide, for example in Japan and Russia, as the technology is more expensive than conventional reactors. Also fast-breeders create even more plutonium as they release energy. This substance could be used to make nuclear weapons, which brings its own problems (see pages 24–25).

Nuclear waste is not a problem when stored properly

For:

Small amounts
There are fairly small amounts – 260,000 tonnes globally – of high-level nuclear waste needing the most careful disposal.

Waste management
The nuclear industry deals with its waste more carefully than most other industries and is also checked by government and international agencies.

The concrete containers stacked in this surface storage facility in La Hague, France, contain spent nuclear fuel waiting to be reprocessed.

Against:

Changing conditions
Containers and storage sites may change over time. For example, salt water could weaken containers, allowing radioactive waste to leak.

Future hazards?
Nuclear waste has only been stored since the 1950s, so how can anyone know how it might be affected by future hazards? Also, by 2030 it is predicted there will be three times as much waste to store awaiting reprocessing as there was in 2010.

Nuclear waste is mostly stored carefully and responsibly at present. However, changes at storage sites into the future could release radiation.

Nuclear accidents

When accidents happen in nuclear reactors or fuel factories, radiation may be released into the environment. Such accidents are rare, and have killed fewer than 100 people since the nuclear power industry began. However, the potential for disaster is huge compared with many other alternative energy resources.

Nuclear meltdown

The two major nuclear power station accidents of the 20th century – Chernobyl, Ukraine, and Three Mile Island, USA – occurred following nuclear **meltdown**. This is when reactors get so hot that they set on fire and damage **containment** buildings built around the reactor to prevent radioactive waste from escaping. The cause of the meltdown in each case was loss of coolant, due to safety systems going wrong. When the fuel rods were not cooled they burnt through the bottom of the reactor. Radiation escaped from Chernobyl in different ways. The hot fuel reacted with water underground and the fire produced a cloud of radioactive smoke and dust, or **fallout**, which spread through the atmosphere. Fallout from Chernobyl spread all across Europe, but most fell nearest the station. Around 2,000 local children developed cancers, many as a result of drinking milk from cows that had fed on contaminated grass. Fortunately most children were cured.

The abandoned fairground in Pripyat, a town near the Chernobyl nuclear power station. Pripyat was deserted after the meltdown owing to high levels of radiation from fallout.

Safety first

Supporters of nuclear power point out that accidents happened in the past because safety standards were lower than they are today. For example, containment buildings are typically made of concrete and steel several metres thick today, whereas Chernobyl was an old reactor built with thin steel containment. Nuclear power stations employ highly trained workers and use lots of sensors to measure temperatures and radiation levels in order to shut down systems if things go wrong.

The control room of a nuclear power station has lots of dials and lights that automatically warn workers when sensors throughout the station detect any problems.

CASE STUDY   Fukushima accident

On 11 March 2011 a major earthquake under the ocean off Japan caused a giant tsunami that inundated around 560 square kilometres of the country. It killed over 19,000 people and destroyed or damaged millions of buildings. The tsunami also flooded three coastal nuclear power stations at Fukushima. This cut off power needed to cool the reactors and their nuclear cores mostly melted in just three days. Emergency response teams including robots managed to lower temperatures in the reactors and prevent meltdown. The Japanese government was so worried by the radiation threat that they evacuated around 160,000 people from the surrounding area. The reactors remain shut down, scientists have cleaned up any radioactive waste released and no people have died as a result of the reactor accident, but many still stay away partly because of fears about their health.

Other impacts of nuclear power

Other impacts of using nuclear power include pollution and land destruction. Uranium mining causes water and some air pollution, and land is destroyed when mines and power stations are built.

Water problems

Surface and underground uranium mining creates large amounts of waste rock, and processing yellowcake creates lakes of liquid waste. The waste contains uranium and other hazardous metals and may be washed away by rainwater or spill into soil, groundwater and rivers. This causes long-lasting water pollution. Radioactive substances can also evaporate from the tops of waste ponds leading to fallout. For example, villagers living near uranium mines in Kyrgyzstan, receive radiation doses around 40 times higher than recommended safe limits, mostly from eating food grown on polluted land.

Overuse of water for solution mining is another problem. In Australia, a generally dry country, 35 million litres of water is being extracted from the Great Artesian Basin groundwater source each day by a uranium mining company. Falling levels in the basin are causing freshwater springs to dry up, threatening different types of wildlife that live there, and leaving less water for farmers to irrigate farmland.

Large ponds of water containing radioactive waste built up near the Uruvan mine, Colorado, USA, during yellowcake production.

Land and atmosphere

Building any large power station, nuclear or otherwise, involves buying and clearing land for building roads, pylons and other necessary structures. Although nuclear power stations make no greenhouse gases during operation, they are responsible for some pollution caused by the vehicles used for the transportation of nuclear fuel and waste, and mining equipment such as pumps and diggers. The gases produced may increase in future as mining companies have to process ore containing lower proportions of uranium to supply nuclear fuel because the best uranium sources have run out.

CASE STUDY

Heat from Turkey Point

Nuclear power stations release warm water into the environment and this has an impact on wildlife. At Turkey Point nuclear power station, Florida, USA, cold river water is used to cool steam from turbines. The warmed water enters a network of canals to cool before being reused in the station. Near the stations warm water has killed areas of turtle grass, home to animals such as crabs. However, the heat has had a positive impact on a population of the endangered American crocodile. The warm water increases the survival rate of young crocodiles and the banks between the protected channels are good nesting sites. Breeding success has increased the numbers of crocodiles near the stations. In 2012 they made up over one quarter of the total US crocodile population.

American crocodiles are endangered owing to hunting and loss of coastal habitat. Areas inaccessible to hunters, such as Turkey Point, are vital refuges where populations can grow.

The cost of nuclear power

Setting up any power station is expensive. There is the cost of machinery to generate electricity and cabling to take it to consumers. Once the station is operating there are ongoing costs of buying fuel, paying workers, carrying out safety checks and dealing with waste. It also costs money to dismantle, or **decommission**, a power station at the end of its life.

Comparing costs

The average cost of building a nuclear power station is around £3500 per kilowatt (kW) of electricity produced, around twice that of a new coal power station. The extra expense is because of safety features needed to reduce radiation hazards. However, comparing the costs of using different energy resources is not always straightforward. For example, global prices of fuels such as uranium, coal or gas vary widely according to supply and demand. Nevertheless, many power companies say nuclear power electricity is similar in cost to fossil fuel power or hydroelectric power, and cheaper than renewables per kW per hour, on average.

This part of an old nuclear reactor has been coated in blue film to seal in the radioactive dust before it is transported away to another location for decommissioning.

Decommissioning

Nuclear reactors last for between 30 to 60 years. After this, they are decommissioned because repairing them is too expensive, their structure has weakened or because steel parts of the reactor have become radioactive. During decommissioning, power stations are dismantled and radioactive dust is cleared up by specialist workers. The most radioactive parts of the reactor may be collected together and encased in thick concrete.

If the nuclear power station is removed, radioactive land is cleaned for example by growing plants such as sunflowers that take in radioactive substances through their roots. Decommissioning is time-consuming and often dangerous work and can cost power companies as much as or more than building nuclear power stations in the first place. Power companies usually pay for decommissioning.

Let's discuss   Is nuclear power cheaper than coal power?

Yes:

Global warming cost
If coal power companies had to pay for the effects of global warming, such as failed crops, this could double the cost of their electricity. Nuclear power stations themselves produce no greenhouse gases.

Longer lifespans
Nuclear power companies are upgrading turbines and other parts to make them last longer. This makes generating costs even lower and delays expensive decommissioning.

No:

Hidden costs
Disposing of nuclear waste is very expensive. It costs up to £200,000 per cubic metre for the highest-level waste and building safe storage sites can cost billions.

Shutdowns
Nuclear power stations are shut down for safety reasons when problems occur, for example in hot weather if cooling water is too warm, and then the price per kW produced rises.

Nuclear power is cheaper than coal power, because the costs of global warming are probably higher than the costs of dealing with radioactive waste and safely operating nuclear power stations.

Encouraging nuclear power

Following the Chernobyl meltdown in the late 1980s, many countries looked for alternatives to nuclear power. However, in the first decades of the 21st century more governments are encouraging nuclear power because it doesn't increase global warming and because they have been slow to develop enough renewable power to meet their electricity needs.

Subsidizing to cut greenhouse gases

Many of the world's governments have made agreements to cut the amounts of greenhouse gases their country's produce in order to slow global warming. In order to maintain electricity supply to their populations, these governments **subsidize**, or pay money, to encourage power technologies that release less greenhouse gas than fossil fuels. These include 'green' technologies, such as wind, solar and hydroelectricity. Governments subsidize the nuclear industry for this reason in different ways, such as paying for scientists to research into new reactor designs and lending money to install nuclear technology.

Governments may encourage nuclear power in order to guarantee the electricity their populations need without the environmental and future supply issues of using fossil fuels.

Subsidies for nuclear power may also help other industries. In 2009 there were long delays in building some reactors because only a few factories in the world, in Japan and France, can make certain specialist parts. Therefore, some countries such as the USA hope to encourage their industries to make reactors. One idea is to modify closed car factories and retrain car workers so they can produce simple reactors on assembly lines. This could make nuclear power stations cheaper to build and encourage power companies to use this energy resource more.

CASE STUDY   Finland's nuclear future

In 2002 the Finnish government voted to build the world's largest nuclear power station at Olkiluoto, western Finland, by 2009. The idea was to generate enough electricity to power the growing timber and paper industries vital to the economy and to meet Finland's greenhouse gas targets. It is being built for the Finnish state nuclear power company by Areva (France) and Siemens (Germany). However, the station will not now be completed until 2016 and first power will reach the electrical grid by 2018. The project is expected to cost over twice the initial estimates. One reason for the delay and extra cost is that inspectors found that coolant pipes built in the reactor had to be replaced as they were welded so badly. There were also problems with electronic safety monitors. The extra cost, which will need to be paid through taxes, has led many Finnish people to question the decision to build Olkiluoto.

Electricity from the finished Olkiluoto nuclear power station is important in Finland's plans to grow its economy.

Protesting against nuclear power

Governments face public protest over the building of new nuclear power stations because of safety concerns. Many protestors are troubled by the links between nuclear power and nuclear weapons.

Material for weapons

Plutonium and enriched uranium, with over 90 per cent U235, can be used to make nuclear weapons. Globally, many countries, from the USA to Iran, have the technology to enrich uranium and to reprocess waste fuel, creating plutonium. Some have fast-breeder reactors that can create plutonium, too.

There is also material for new weapons from old weapons. Stockpiles of nuclear missiles were built up during political conflict between USA and Russia in the past. Now the weapons have been dismantled, leaving enough material in store to make thousands of new bombs. Some people fear that terrorists could steal it to make their own weapons.

Monitoring the nuclear industry

Different international groups monitor the nuclear industry to control the spread of nuclear weapon technology. For example, the International Atomic Energy Agency (IAEA) employs inspectors who visit nuclear facilities worldwide to check they are not enriching uranium or collecting plutonium specifically for weapons. Scientists working for IAEA use special equipment to detect whether countries are testing nuclear bombs with test explosions.

Many international charities protest against nuclear power largely because of the lethal threat of nuclear weapons with which it is linked.

Could terrorists target nuclear power stations?

Yes:

Major radioactive source
An average nuclear power station's reactor would release more radiation than a nuclear bomb if it were seriously damaged.

Long-lasting problem
A successful terrorist attack on a reactor or even a cooling pond could release radiation that would remain a problem for decades.

No:

Safety measures
Nuclear power stations are high-security facilities. Workers and emergency services have well-rehearsed evacuation and containment plans.

Tough reactors?
Containment structures of modern reactors are strong enough to withstand a small plane crash, although they could probably not survive a large impact.

Nuclear power companies say they minimize dangers of terrorism by using police and security companies to guard their spent fuel.

Nuclear power stations are possible terrorist targets, but safety measures make this as unlikely as a nuclear accident.

New nuclear technology

Supplies of uranium with the highest proportion of U235 are dwindling fast. The costs of building reactors are increasing and there is public demand for safer reactors. Therefore, scientists are developing new methods of releasing nuclear energy using less fuel, more cheaply and with fewer hazards than older designs.

Pebble-bed reactors

Pebble-bed reactors contain hundreds of thousands of ball-shaped graphite pebbles. Most contain grains of uranium coated in protective layers and the rest act like control rods in controlling the nuclear reaction. The coolant is the gas helium, which heats up and turns a turbine and generator directly, rather than the heat being used to make steam. Therefore, the reactor is 40 per cent more efficient in its use of heat energy than traditional water-cooled reactors. The reactor design is also less complicated and smaller, so it is cheaper to build. Pebbles from the bottom are regularly removed and new ones added at the top, so it should be simpler to operate.

Pebble-bed reactors are being developed in South Africa and China, but there are concerns that the graphite of the pebbles could set alight, exposing the nuclear fuel inside. Radiation could then be released from the reactor.

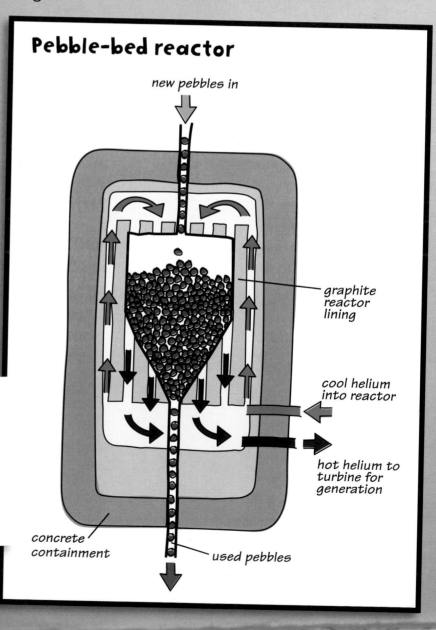

Pebble-bed reactor

new pebbles in

graphite reactor lining

cool helium into reactor

hot helium to turbine for generation

concrete containment

used pebbles

Nuclear fusion

The Sun produces energy by **nuclear fusion** – joining together the nuclei of hydrogen atoms to release energy. Scientists believe they could mimic this in special reactors using hydrogen fuel called deuterium, extracted from seawater, and tritium, extracted from the metal lithium. The problem is that the fuel needs to be incredibly hot or moving very fast to react. Scientists have achieved this with tiny amounts of fuel in laboratories using powerful lasers and magnets. However, so far the machinery has used far more electricity to make fusion happen than the amount it has generated.

magnet

magnet

This fusion reactor is the shape of a ring doughnut. Circular magnets around the outside trap the fuel inside. Here its two halves have been moved apart for maintenance.

CASE STUDY Fusion in France

The first large fusion test reactor is being built in the south of France. It is being paid for by the European Union, the USA, Russia, Japan, China and South Korea. At the heart of the reactor is a 23,000-tonne machine containing 18 vast magnets each bigger than an SUV which will suspend the hydrogen as it fuses. One problem is that the materials necessary to hold the fuel have not yet been invented. For example, the fast-moving neutrons from fusion reactions would make normal stainless steel boil. The French reactor is a testing ground for solving problems in using fusion commercially for generating power. Scientists estimate that the first actual fusion reactors won't be in action until around 2050.

'Fusion is like trying to put the Sun in a box – but we don't know how to make the box.'

Professor Sebastien Balibar, National Research Laboratory, France

The future for nuclear power

Nuclear power has the potential to supply large and constant amounts of electricity in future without increasing global warming. It could be a more expensive but quicker and more dependable way of meeting our electricity needs than renewables, once fossil fuels start to run out or the effects of global warming increase. However, the hazard potential of nuclear power will mean it is always only part of a future energy mix.

More reactors?

Countries from China to Russia are building new reactors and many more are planned in places including India and Indonesia. However, although more reactors will be operational in the next decades, many are approaching the decommissioning age. Most reactors worldwide are around 25 years old, and 73 are 35 years or older. Therefore, overall the nuclear power industry is barely growing. Future nuclear expansion may be helped by the development of smaller, simpler and cheaper reactors and nuclear batteries (see case study). This will make nuclear power an option in places off the electrical grid – the network of cables and pylons connecting power stations to businesses and homes. Examples of off-grid locations include less-developed countries of the world, such as Vietnam, and remote mines or military bases.

The concrete lid is lowered onto a new nuclear reactor in China. The Chinese government plans to massively increase its nuclear power capacity twelve-fold between 2015 and 2030.

Other energy solutions

Nuclear power can only meet part of our energy needs at present. For example, nuclear reactors are too expensive and impractical for safety reasons to use to run vehicles such as aeroplanes and cars. Sources of renewable power will also be important future energy solutions, depending on location. Solar power works best in places with lots of sunlight through the year, while powerful river flows are needed for hydroelectric generation. Many scientists say that a better solution for the future is to use less energy, using machines that work on less electricity or less fuel, and for all of us to become more 'energy conscious'.

CASE STUDY

Nuclear battery factory

Gen4 Energy is a small company with a dream of making nuclear power small and portable! Its Gen4 module is rather like a nuclear battery that could be used at hundreds of off-grid locations worldwide. Each battery contains enough uranium to deliver 25 MW of electricity – enough for about 25,000 US homes – for 10 years. The modules are sealed to contain the waste and radioactive hazard, and cooled using advanced liquid metal moving through pipes. After 10 years the modules can be unearthed and removed safely to factories where the fuel can be replaced – rather like a rechargeable battery! Furthermore the fuel and waste in Gen4 is very difficult to convert into nuclear explosives, so these mini power stations are safer than large nuclear facilities.

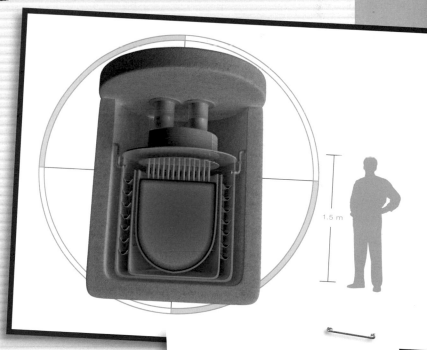

1.5 m

Each battery will contain a sealed mini-nuclear reactor about 2 metres tall and be buried underground.

Nuclear activity

What you need:
• Dominos
• Ruler
• Flat table

Demonstrate a chain reaction

During fission, U235 splits off two neutrons, which in turn strike two U-235 atoms, in a chain reaction. You can simulate this with dominoes!

1 Arrange the dominoes as shown (NB this is a view from above onto the top edges of standing dominoes).

2 Knock over the single domino in front (arrowed) and watch the impact of your action on the other dominoes.

3 Now arrange the dominoes in a straight line – when you knock the first, the others should all fall. This simulates how one splitting atom affects others nearby.

4 Set up the domino line again and place the ruler between two dominoes half-way along the line. How is the ruler acting like a control rod in a reactor?

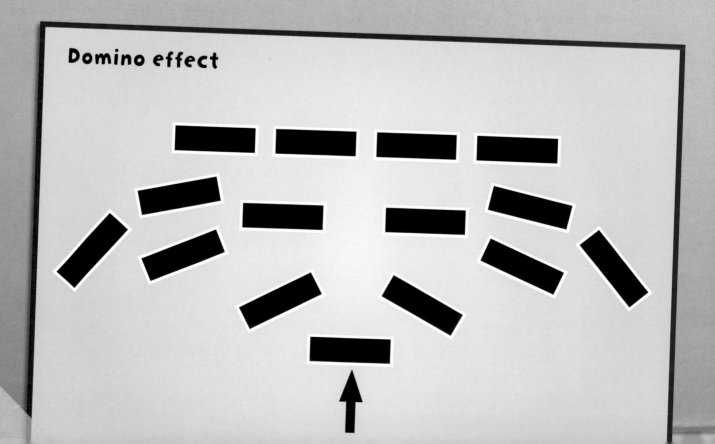

Domino effect

Nuclear topics and glossary

History
- Create a timeline of nuclear power, including its first uses for generating electricity.

Geography
- Could we get rid of nuclear waste by melting it in hot rock many kilometres underground? Research the pros and cons.

Design and Technology
- The radiation hazard symbol is used in campaigns against

nuclear power. Design a symbol to warn others of the global warming hazard.

English
- Create an A4 leaflet persuading villagers why they should accept having a nuclear power station built near their village.

Science
- Research when the Geiger counter was invented and how it works.

Glossary

atmosphere mix of gases surrounding the Earth up to the edge of space.

atom smallest part of an element.

chain reaction sequence of nuclear reactions caused and continued by itself.

condense change from gas to liquid.

containment designed to prevent escape, for example of radiation.

control rod part of nuclear reactor used to slow fission reaction.

coolant liquid or gas used to cool a reactor.

decommission officially stop using, often by taking apart.

enrich improve quality or proportion of one component.

fallout radioactive dust.

fast-breeder reactor type of nuclear reactor that produces plutonium through reactions.

fossil fuel fuel such as coal formed over millions of years from the remains of living things.

gamma ray high-energy rays from some radioactive substances.

generator machine that converts mechanical into electrical energy.

global warming increase in the average temperature of the atmosphere and oceans.

greenhouse gas gas such as carbon dioxide that stores heat in the atmosphere.

kinetic energy energy produced by movement.

mechanical energy energy of moving machine parts.

meltdown serious accident when nuclear reactor releases radiation.

neutron tiny atomic particle with no charge.

non-renewable describes an energy resource that is not replaced as it is used.

nuclear energy energy released from nuclei of radioactive elements.

nuclear fission splitting nuclei.

nuclear fusion combining nuclei.

nucleus part of atom containing particles giving most of its mass.

plutonium type of radioactive element.

pollution harmful substances that make air, water or soil less safe to use or live in.

radiation powerful and dangerous rays.

radioactive releasing harmful radiation.

reaction chemical change when two or more substances combine.

reactor structure where nuclear fuel reacts.

renewable describes an energy resource that can be used without running out.

reprocess recycle used nuclear fuel to separate out useful fuel from waste.

solution mining process by which minerals are extracted by dissolving in water.

subsidize pay to support something and encourage its success.

turbine machine changing the push of steam or other substance into rotation.

uranium type of radioactive substance.

yellowcake processed uranium ore.

Find out more and index

Find out more

Websites

http://scienceclub.nei.org/scienceclub/
nuclearworld.html
  Discover what makes nuclear power
  stations safe, and how to deal with
  nuclear waste at this interesting site.

http://tonto.eia.doe.gov/kids/energy.
cfm?page=nonrenewable_home-basics
  Compare non-renewable energy
  resources by exploring this useful
  website. Other parts of the site deal
  with renewables, too.

Books

Nuclear Power (Our World) by Sarah
  Levete (Franklin Watts, 2008)

Nuclear Power (Energy Sources) by Neil
  Morris (Franklin Watts, 2008)

Nuclear Power: Is it too Risky? (World
  Energy Issues) by Jim Pipe (Franklin
  Watts, 2010)

Index